GROWTH OF PHALAENOPSIS HANDBOOK

Indoor Phalaenopsis Orchid Care and Growing Instructions

COURTNEY JOYER

Table of Contents

CHAPTER ONE

PROSPEROUS GROWTH OF PHALAENOPSIS

Indoor Phalaenopsis Orchid Care and Growing Instructions

Only the tropical regions of Asia and Australia are home to the Phalaenopsis orchld, which is best known for brightening up

U.S. homes. It is nearly impossible to grow these exotic flowers outside of North America. Many orchid varieties are available, but Phalaenopsis orchids remain the most popular because they're a good choice for novices.

This type of orchid has multiple flower buds on its axils, which can bloom for up to a month or more if properly cared for. The arching branches of their long-lasting flowers open sequentially. More than 20 flowers can grow on a single multi-branching flower spike, and each flower can last for weeks.

Although Phalaenopsis Orchids are known for having a complicated name, they're actually quite simple to care for. For as long as you follow a few simple guidelines, they'll continue to bloom beautifully.

With its long stems, delicate wing-like flowers, and deep green foliage, this plant is a beautiful addition to any home or office. A popular gift is Phalaenopsis Orchids because of their long-lasting nature. Cut flowers from Fig and Bloom typically last for one to two weeks, depending on the variety and the climate in which they are grown. You can't go wrong with a Phalaenopsis Orchid if you're looking for something that will last longer. Gift recipients can expect to enjoy this low-maintenance plant for several months to come. It's entirely possible that you'll want one for yourself as well!

As many of our florists love these plants, they also have them in their personal gardens. To help you care for your

Phalaenopsis Orchid, we've put together this comprehensive guide.

Common Name Phalaenopsis, the orchid of the moth

Plant Family Phalaenopsis

Family Orchidaceae

Herbaceous and perennial

Can Phalaenopsis Orchids Be Grown Indoors?

As long as they are kept in the right conditions, Phalaenopsis orchids can bloom for months at a time. In tropical areas, these orchids can be found growing on tree trunks and branches. As a result, it's best to create conditions that are as close to real as possible. Finding the right combination of humidity, temperature, light, and airflow is essential for healthy growth.

Sunlight

The leaves of Phalaenopsis will burn if they are exposed to direct sunlight. The orchid can be kept in a south or east-facing window with some direct light during the winter. Keep your orchid's growth even by rotating it from time to time. Light green leaves can be produced by a plant that receives adequate light. Leaves with a pink or reddish tinge develop along the leaf margins and eventually turn yellow when exposed to too little light or too much light, respectively.

Illumination provided by artificial means

Supplemental grow lights can also be used if natural light isn't enough for the plant. Fluorescent tubes (40 or 74 watts, depending on length) are the preferred lighting for orchids, and the Phalaenopsis should be placed 12 inches beneath the light.

CHAPTER TWO

Measurements of Air Quality:

In order to thrive, Phalaenopsis prefers temperatures ranging from 75 to 85 degrees Fahrenheit. They can, however, adapt to temperatures between 65 and 70 degrees Fahrenheit. Heat and humidity both increase the plant's need for turbulent airflow in order to prevent rot, fungus, and disease, so as the temperature rises, so does this requirement. In rooms where orchids are being grown, many successful orchid growers keep a ceiling fan or a stationary fan constantly running.

Orchids, like other flowering plants, enjoy the contrast between day and night temperatures. In order for the plant to produce a flower spike, it needs several nights with temperatures below 55 degrees Fahrenheit to do so.

Watering

"Monopodial" refers to the fact that the orchids of Phalaenopsis grow from a single stem.

Sympodial (or branching) orchids have large pseudobulbs that store water, so this plant is less tolerant of drought.

Plants need weekly or whenever their exposed roots turn silvery white watering during their growing season (about once a week). Give the orchid plenty of time to absorb the water by rinsing the plant, bark, and aerial roots three or four times in about 10 minutes. Before putting it back in its window, make sure it's completely empty. The plant's stem should never be submerged in water.

The new leaves will rot, and the plant will die as a result. The roots should turn from silver to a pale green color after being watered. Watering can be reduced to every other week when flowers are in bloom. Overwatering and excessive moisture in the growing medium are the most common causes of root and stem rot in Phalaenopsis orchids.

Fertilizer

It's a good idea to feed your orchid every third or fourth week during the growing season. Prevent excessive foliage and lack of blooms by not feeding during the fall, winter and spring (flowering season). To encourage a flower spike, some growers like to give the plant a "bloom booster" in September or October.

Maintenance and Pruning

Pruning mature orchids once a year, after the blooms have faded, is recommended. You can encourage more blooms by cutting the stem back one inch above its node with clean scissors or a knife. Alternatively, you can carefully remove spent flowers by letting the plant do its own thing. Keep an eye out for diseased roots that are either brown or mushy; remove them.

If your orchid's roots are protruding above the soil, this is perfectly normal. Don't remove the aerial roots. You don't have to do anything.

Phalaenopsis Orchid Species

Phalaenopsis orchids are a genus of about 60 distinct species. Hybridization of these plants has resulted in thousands of varieties, from the classic white hybrid moth orchid to jewel-like miniatures with clouds of yellow and candy pink blooms. To name just a few grower favorites:

Liodoro's Phalaenopsis has wavy green leaves and star-shaped flowers in shades of pink and purple. The height of this plant is 19 inches.

Large, 2.5-inch, pink and purple flowers with dark green variegated leaves are found in Phalaenopsis schilleriana. This variety's stems can produce up to 200 flowers per stem.

• Phalaenopsis stuartiana can grow up to 30 inches tall and has white flowers with yellow and red dots.

As a result of their smaller stature, MiniPhalaenopsis require less water and come in a variety of flower colors.

Size and Shape

Phalaenopsis, like all epiphytic orchids, requires well-drained containers with plenty of drainage holes to ensure it never sits in standing water.

Most Phalaenopsis can be grown in an azalea pot with a diameter of 4 to 6 inches, and this is the maximum size in which they are ever planted. Both plastic and terra cotta pots work fine as long as they have good drainage.

A Potting Soil and a Drainage

When found in their natural habitat, moth orchids can be found growing on the branches of trees. As a result, they are known as an epiphyte—a plant that needs a host but is not parasitic. The bark of the fir tree, redwood chips, or Monterey pine chips is commonly used in the manufacture of potting mixes for potted orchids in an attempt to mimic these natural conditions. Perlite, sphagnum moss, charcoal, and coconut husk chips are common additions to bark potting media that aid in water retention for orchids. A commercial orchid potting mix is also available for purchase. The roots of Phalaenopsis need to be well-ventilated, as they cannot thrive in a suffocating environment.

Taking care of Phalaenopsis Orchids in the garden

Spring is the best time to repot Phalaenopsis orchids because the blooms have finished and roots are starting to show through the pot. In most cases, adult Phalaenopsis do not require repotting for at least two years after they are established in a container. Add an inch or two to the pot's diameter and disinfect it with a mild bleach solution before using it (orchids are very sensitive to bacteria). Make sure to thoroughly clean your hands and any tools you plan on using. Wait for the pot to dry completely before adding an orchid potting media to it. If any brown roots remain, gently cut them off and place the orchid in a new pot filled with moistened bark medium. The roots should be gently pushed into the soil. Make sure to mist your plants every day until you see new roots sprouting from the ground.

CHAPTER THREE

Propagating

Seed propagation is possible, but the process is lengthy and expensive, so it's best left to professional growers. A keiki is an orchid's naturally produced "baby," which home growers can replant to multiply their moth orchids. On old or new flower spikes, keikis appear, which are identical copies of the parent. Taking the keiki from the parent plant and putting it in its own pot can be done after about a year.

From a keiki, you can grow orchids.

a pot, spray bottle, flower scissors, alcohol wipes, and orchid-specific potting medium all in one location.

After a year, the keiki should be about three inches tall, have two or three leaves of its own, and have developed several strong roots.

The alcohol wipes can be used to clean the scissors' blades, and then carefully remove the keiki from the parent plant, being careful not to damage the roots.

You can leave some of its roots exposed, as long as the bark medium is moistened before you plant it in its own pot.

5. Mist the baby plant with water every day until it is well-established. a.)

FAQ

• Are Phalaenopsis orchids susceptible to disease?

There are a number of fungal conditions that can affect them. These include leaf spots and fungal decay. In most cases, the affected part of the plant (leaf, root, or flower) can be removed, and the plant can be treated with a fungicide. The good news is that all of this can be avoided if the soil is kept in good condition.

• Why do my orchids' leaves have wrinkles?

Under-watering and/or a lack of humidity are the most likely causes of wrinkled leaves on your orchid. Don't let the pot sit in the water when adding a pebble tray to increase humidity.

Orchids are frequently attacked by a variety of pests.

Because they are usually grown indoors, Phalaenopsis orchids rarely have insect problems. It is still possible for scale and mealy bugs to enter an orchid that has been grown outside or in a greenhouse. Insecticide soap can be used to treat most pest problems.

• **Why are my orchids losing their buds?**

Orchids can suffer from bud blast, in which the flower buds fall off before they have a chance to bloom. Temperature, humidity, moisture, or fertilizer fluctuations are the most common culprits. The likelihood of issues arising should be reduced if optimal growing conditions are maintained.

Phalaenopsis orchids won't bloom again, what should I do?

Phalaenopsis orchids bloom only once a year in the wild. With a few simple steps, you can get them to bloom every six months indoors. Trim the brown stem to a height of no more than three inches after the last bloom has fallen. Continue to feed your plant a diluted liquid fertilizer in order to encourage growth and blooms, as you normally would. A new leaf on the stem means the plant is ready to rebloom. Relocate your orchid to a cooler location with bright indirect sunlight and temperatures between 55 and 65 degrees Fahrenheit. If you keep your orchid in this cooler environment for a month, it should bloom again.

THE END